ONCE A SOURDOUGH, ALWAYS A SOURDOUGH!

ONCE A SOURDOUGH, ALWAYS A SOURDOUGH!

By Sherry Fox Clark

Ⓜ
Memoir
BOOKS
Chico, CA

ONCE A SOURDOUGH, ALWAYS A SOURDOUGH!
Copyright © 2015 by Sherry Fox Clark
ISBN: 978-1-937748-19-7
Library of Congress Control Number: 2015900593
First Edition

Memoir Books
An Imprint of Heidelberg Graphics
2 Stansbury Court
Chico, California 95928

Title page photo: K Arthur Fox

TABLE OF CONTENTS

ARCTIC

Pt. Hope — Point Hope

Endicott — Range

Kotzebue Sd.

Noatak R.

Koluk R.

Ft. Yukon

Bering Strait

Seward Penin.

Council

Peavy

Yukon

Tanana

Rampart

Circle

Fairbank

Koyukuk R.

Hills

Nulato

Yukon R.

Atwood

Tanana

Nome

Solomon

Norton Sd.

Pt. Dall

Unalakleet

St. Michael

Anvik

Mt. McKinley

Mt. Forakr

Mt. Sanford

Mt. Wrangell

K

Yukon R.

NELSON

Kuskokwim R.

S

Tyonek

Sunrise Valdez

Seward

Kenai

L. Clark

Iliamna L.

Koggiung

Kaldovia

Kuchue

Igagik

Bristol Bay

Ugushik

Kuskokwim B.

Alaska Penin.

Shelikof St.

Kat

Afognak

Kodiak

Aleutian

GULF

Afognak

AL

Cooka Inlet

SEMIDI IS.

TRINITY IS.

UNIM

NASAN IS.

SHUMAGIN IS.

SANNAK IS.

ALASKA

A

PACIFIC

S

NDS

DEDICATION

"Sourdough," a name given to fellow pioneers and miners of the early 19th Century in the far North Alaskan Territory, (a reference to the leavening used in bread making when yeast is not available.)

This title was used by my grandmother, Stella Holmes Fox, lovingly referring to her lifelong friends and companions while telling myself and my two sisters stories of adventures our grandfather Edward A. Fox, our father K Arthur Fox, and his younger sister Lola L. Fox, experienced while living and gold mining in the Alaskan Territory.

Thanks to my grandmother this book was made possible because of her foresight to photograph, journal, and save many pieces of memorabilia to pass on and chronicle this piece of our nations' history.

With great pride I present this book as a tribute to my grandparents and others that had the strength of conviction to brave the wilderness and hardships of the Far North Alaskan Territory to search for gold during the early 1900s to make a better life for their families.

—Sherry Fox Clark

Stella J. Holmes, 1907

ONCE A SOURDOUGH, ALWAYS A SOURDOUGH!

My name is Stella Holmes Fox and I became a "Sourdough." I was born Stella Josephine Holmes in Ada, Minnesota in April 1879. I was one of six children, four girls and two boys. My father was a foreman on the Great Northern Railroad while it was being built connecting the Great Lakes area of the Midwest and the Pacific Northwest.

At the age of three we moved to Plainfield, Iowa, where I finished High School and decided to become a teacher.

I started out teaching in a country school house like my sister Chassie, who was two and a half years older. We received $25.00 per month for teaching and doing our own janitorial work. Our father owned an old white horse with a lame foreleg, so we couldn't go very fast, but we hitched him up to a wagon to get to and from school every day. Chassie taught at a school two miles from our home, but I taught in one that was four miles away. I would drop her off and pick her up on my way home. Chassie was sickly, but I could harness and hitch up a horse in three minutes! I paid a farmer ten cents a month to put our horse in his pasture near the school.

Stella, (one year old.)

Stella, bottom right with father, brothers & sisters.

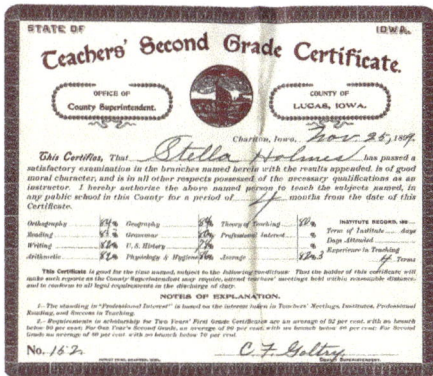

Stella's Iowa teaching certificate.

Stella and her students.

I taught school for four years from age 18 to 22. I learned a lot from my older sister, as she was highly regarded by many as a wonderful teacher. Unfortunately she died at age 26 of tuberculosis. Nearly all families were affected by the dreaded disease at that time, but poor Chassie was the only one in our family to contract T.B. We were very close and I missed her very much.

My mother died of pneumonia in 1900, when I was 21 years old. By 1904 my father broke up housekeeping, sold our family home and went to live with his son, my brother Ade, in Medford, Oregon. I decided to move also, so I went first to the 1904 St. Louis World's Fair, then on to California where my mother had family in Pasadena.

I couldn't teach school in California without attending Normal College, and, as I had little money, I tried my hand in various other ventures. One of which was demonstrating newborn incubators in what you might call a carnival side show. This was in San Francisco at the Chutes Amusement park at Golden Gate Park, later named Playland By The Sea. This amusement park was famous for its original "Shoot The Chutes", an exciting water slide boat ride that was a major attraction for many years. They had a Ferris wheel, roller coaster, in addition to other amusements. A young boy stood out front of the baby incubator attraction calling to the passing crowd, "come in to see this new invention called a "Baby Incubator"!

Stella demonstrating baby incubators.

Another woman and I would dress in nurses' uniforms demonstrating the incubators with premature babies in them to the public that had entered for ten cents each.

We received $9.00 per week, which was very good wages at the time, especially considering I had taught school for $25.00 per month! It sounds strange today, but at the time it was quite a curiosity. This, I found out years later, as a public attraction, was not limited to San Francisco, California, but other cities around the country as well, including one in Coney Island, New York, that remained an attraction until 1941.

While in San Francisco I also worked in a millenery shop making ladies' hats, and also for a time in a photography studio. My younger brother K followed me to California and we lived and worked together in a photo studio for a year or so. This experience became very valuable later, making the photos in this story possible.

Stella and brother K Holmes.

In 1907 I met my future husband, Edward A. Fox. His sister Rose was an acquaintance of mine. He was an unassuming, quiet bachelor, a kind man, five years my senior, and a successful gold miner, born Oct.11, 1874 in Racine, Wisconsin.

Edwards sister Rose Fox and their brother Arthur Fox.

Edward A. Fox, 1907.

Edward began his Alaska adventures with his brother Arthur Fox in 1897 at the age of 23 where they braved the Chilkoot Trail together to the Yukon Territory, a very dangerous undertaking. This trail led from the port city of Skagway to the Klondike gold rush fields of Dawson City, Yukon Territory. Every man or woman was only allowed into the Canadian Territory at the top of the pass if they had fees to enter and carried a ton of provisions each, which they believed to be enough to last a year. This took many trips up and down at the rate of approximately 50 60 pounds per trip. Later, by the time we met, his brother Arthur had settled in Eastern Oregon.

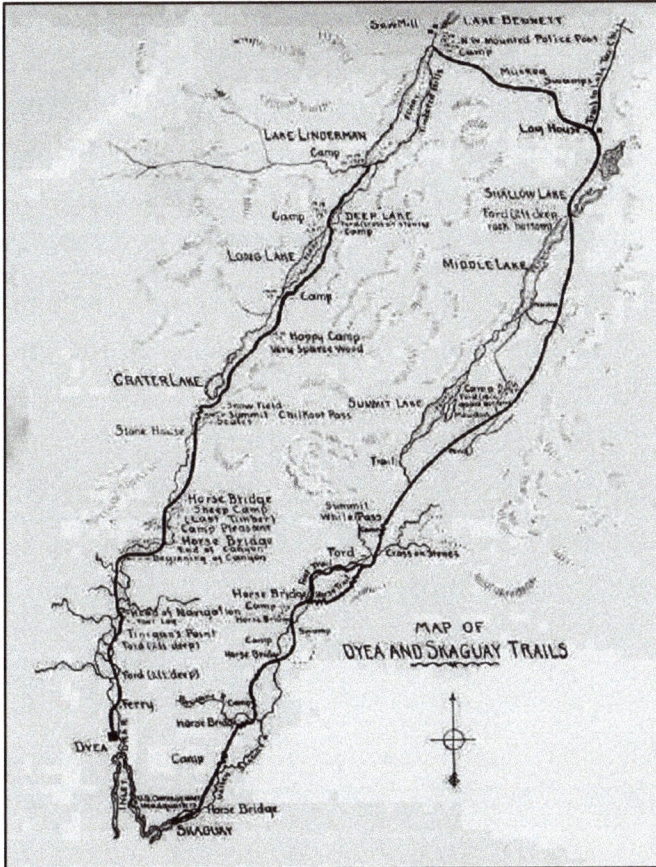

The Seattle Post Intelligencer published this map to the gold fields in 1897. It shows the Dyea (Chilkoot Pass) trail on the left and the Skagway (White Pass) trail on the left. The two trails meet at the top of the map at Lake Bennett.

Photograph courtesy of Special Collections Division, University of Washington Libraries.

MAP OF DYEA AND SKAGUAY TRAILS

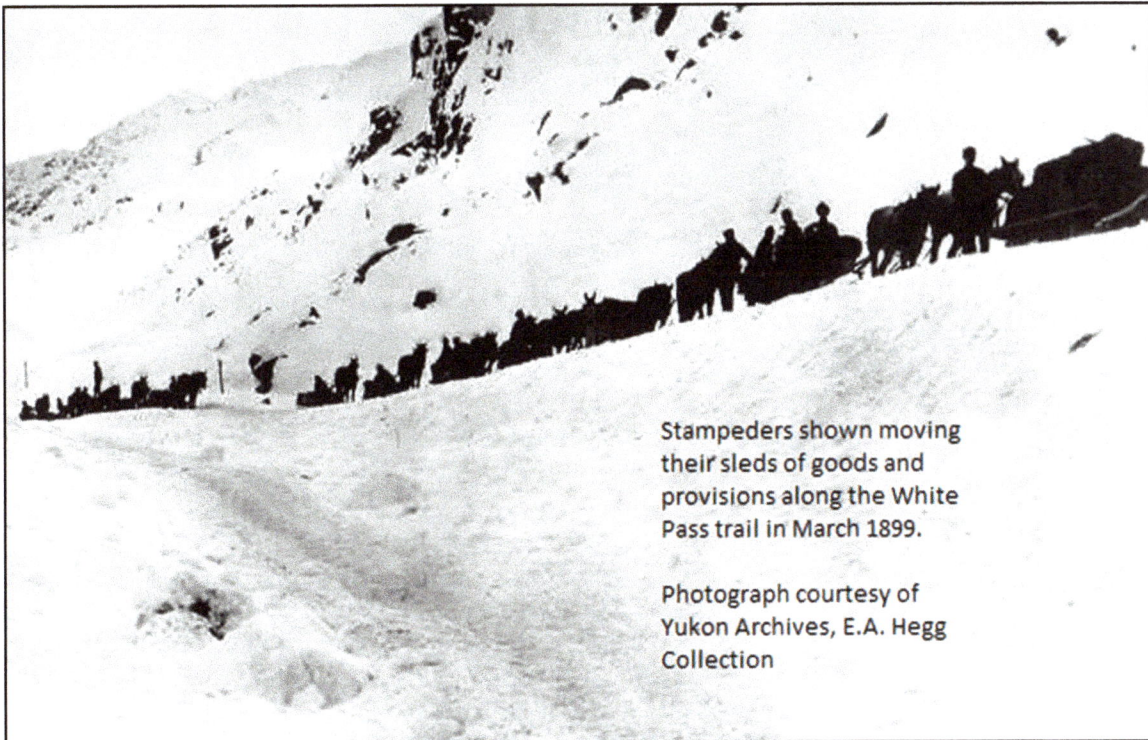

Stampeders shown moving their sleds of goods and provisions along the White Pass trail in March 1899.

Photograph courtesy of Yukon Archives, E.A. Hegg Collection

We courted that winter of 1907, and became engaged. He said that we could not marry right away as he did not have enough money. He would be returning to the Alaskan gold fields that spring.

That June, another girl and I had our first automobile ride with Edward to Seattle so he could catch a ship back to Alaska. I'm not sure of the make of the car, but it was open and had the brake on the outside. I do remember that we had to crank it to get it started. People would come out to look at the car, which was quite a curiosity in 1908!

Edward went aboard the vessel *Ohio* in Seattle, Washington to travel north. This proved to be an arduous voyage as the *Ohio* was caught in the ice for 40 days before they finally arrived at their destination. They were reduced to two meals a day as they ran short on food. Finally they reached Nome and I received a letter from Edward.

Vessel *OHIO* caught in the ice for 40 days, spring of 1908.

We corresponded for the next couple of years as he continued making his mining expeditions to the Alaska wilderness. Shown is a postcard that he mailed on the Russian side of the Bering Strait on his way up North that spring, arriving one year later in California, by way of the Trans-Siberian Railroad, bearing a Russian stamp.

Edward returned and we wed Nov. 16, 1910, in Medford, Oregon, where my brother Ade was a Baptist minister. Here is a clipping from a local newspaper stating that "Edward A. Fox, a prosperous miner from Alaska had returned to claim his bride and return to the Far North."

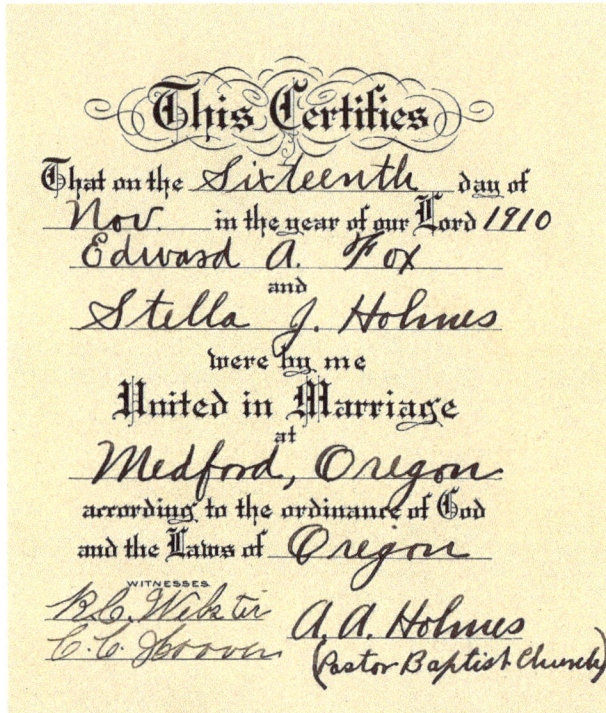

This Certifies

That on the _Sixteenth_ day of _Nov._ in the year of our Lord _1910_ _Edward A. Fox_ and _Stella J. Holmes_ were by me United in Marriage at _Medford, Oregon_ according to the ordinance of God and the Laws of _Oregon_

WITNESSES
R. C. Webster
C. C. Hoover

A. A. Holmes
(Pastor Baptist Church)

COMES LONG WAY TO WED

EDWARD FOX, ALASKAN, CLAIMS MISS HOLMES AS BRIDE

Sister of Baptist Pastor—Marriage at Latter's Home Last Evening—Will Reside in Far North.

It was a long distance which Edward A. Fox came to claim a bride, being a recent arrival from Candle, Alaska, which is in the Arctic regions far beyond Nome. Last evening Miss Stella J. Holmes, a sister of the Rev. Adrian A. Holmes, became his bride and next summer—their announcements fixing it on June 11, 1911 —they will be at home to their friends at Candle, Alaska.

The parlors of the Baptist minister, at 443 South Central avenue, were beautifully decorated for this interesting occasion, having a profusion of chrysanthemums, evergreens and laurels appropriately arranged on walls and trappings. A gathering of closest friends of the young people and their relatives witnessed the event.

At 8 o'clock the bride, attended by her sister-in-law, Mrs. Holmes, as matron of honor, and the groom, with Charles C. Hoover, as best man, made their appearance before the happy assemblage. The brother-pastor spoke the words that united the pair for life. It was a ring ceremony and a very pretty one.

The guests were: Mr. and Mrs. H. W. Whetsel, Mr. and Mrs. Harry H. Tuttle, Mr. and Mrs. S. L. Bennett, Mr. and Mrs. R. C. Webster, Dr. and Mrs. R. W. Stearns, Mr. and Mrs. H. C. Garnett, Mrs. R. S. King, Miss Mabel E. Collins, Mr. D. M. Reid and Mr. Charles C. Hoover.

The bride for the past six months has resided in Medford at the home of her brother and sister-in-law. The groom is a prosperous Alaskan who is interested in mines of the north. They will remain here a few days after which they will depart for Seattle. They will remain there until spring when they will take one of the earliest boats for their northern home.

We spent that winter in Seattle and Edward took the June 1ˢᵗ boat for Nome and walked overland to Candle Creek, (inland and North of Kotzebue, above the Arctic Circle), a distance of some 140 miles overland, to get there in time to get a gold mining claim. I stayed in Seattle to take the 2ⁿᵈ boat to Nome.

Candle Creek was on the northern side of the Seward Peninsula, located on the Kiwalik River, approximately seven miles from Kiwalik in Kotzebue Sound.

Soon after the discovery of gold at Nome there was active prospecting over much of the more readily accessible streams of Seward Peninsula and Candle Creek was staked during July 1901. Shortly after the first strike the town of Candle sprang up and within a few months there were over 1,000 residents. By the time I arrived in the spring of 1911 the population had dwindled to around 100 persons.

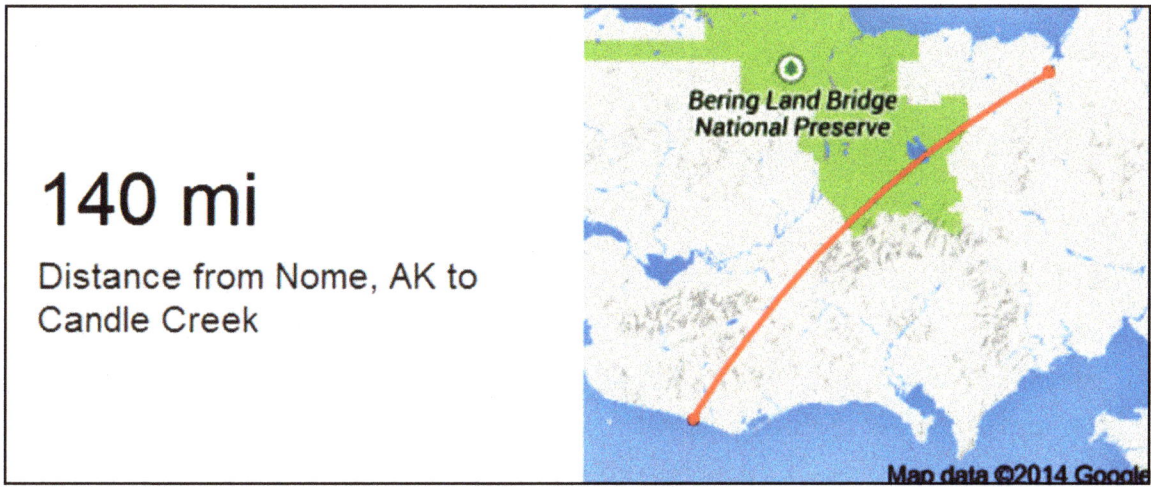

140 mi

Distance from Nome, AK to Candle Creek

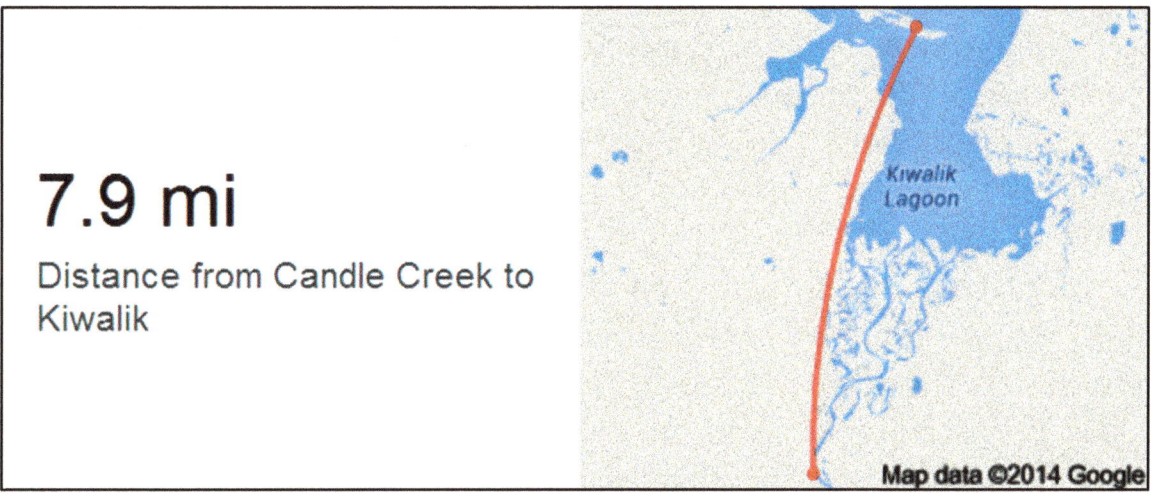

7.9 mi

Distance from Candle Creek to Kiwalik

Candle Creek, Alaska, when I arrived spring of 1911.

When I arrived in Candle Creek in the spring of 1911 supplies and passengers were carried up the river in shallow draft power scows. At normal or low stages of water, if a south wind was blowing; considerable difficulty could be experienced in reaching Candle by boat. The day that I arrived, the river was so low the boat I had taken from the coast could not get all the way up the creek, so the engineer carried me ashore and I walked a mile to town. This was no easy matter considering the boggy tundra grass that grew in large clumps that your feet would slip off of, in addition to struggling along in a long dress, many petticoats and high heeled leather boots!

That first night we slept in a house my husband had bought from a friend, which was not more then a rough shack with a pot bellied stove. There was no timber in the vicinity of Candle, so local coal was used for heating our homes as well as for steaming the permafrost in the mining process. This house eventually became our summer home.

Our first home in Candle Creek, Alaska (summer town home.)

My kitchen in Candle.

The next day we went to an old log cabin and got a dirty old mattress, which had been left behind by a previous resident. I took this mattress apart, washed the wool and made it into a quilt for us.

Of the roughly 100 residents there were only 11 women. They were all very nice and welcoming to me and gave me things for our home. Most of these women became lifelong friends.

Local native Inuit group.

Candle Creek schoolchildren.

When settling in such a small and remote community you learn to rely on each other in all things. In this remote wilderness just surviving can be difficult, but working in underground mining can be an unbelievable challenge. In order to survive the cold temperatures we had to learn from the local Native Inuit people and dress like them. Some of their women were available to help in the home and with the children. I also taught their children in our little school house.

One year after arriving in Alaska, my son K Arthur was born, May 21, 1912, who we named after my youngest brother K, (which was not an abbreviation) and after Edward's younger brother Arthur, followed by my daughter Lola five years later, March 7, 1917. In the delivery of my son I was attended by a midwife, but by the time my daughter was born, we had a new hospital building and a doctor. My daughter was a Downs Syndrome child, which made life a little more difficult. We were happy, however, since we didn't know any different.

(Top left) Native Inuit after the reindeer race. (Top right) Fairhaven Hospital. (Center) Native Inuit on the river. (Bottom) Candle Creek, Alaska, Fairhaven District, 1912.

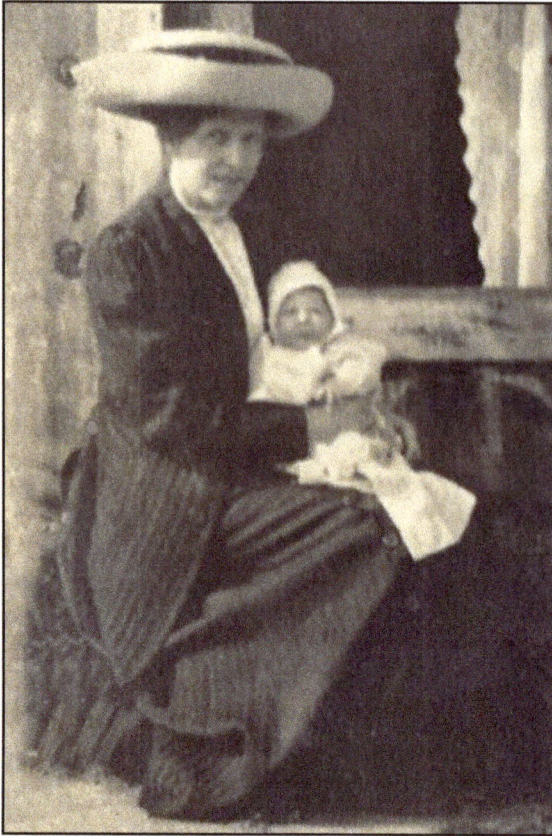

Stella & K Arthur Fox, three months.

K Arthur, ten months

K Arthur, three months

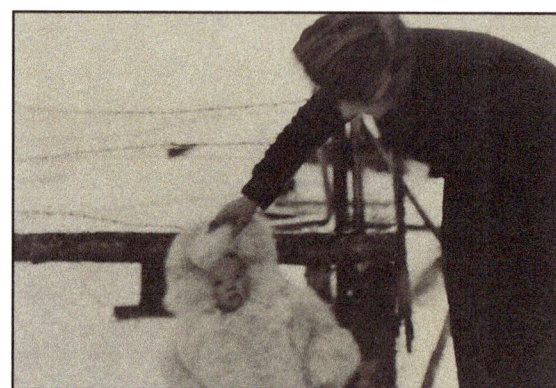

Stella & K Arthur, 10 months.

We traded with the Indians for furs we needed for bedding, parkas, pants and boots. They were glad to trade, and there was always plenty of game for our men to shoot. My son K Arthur learned at a very young age to be an excellent marksman and willow ptarmigan, a native fowl similar to a grouse, were plentiful.

Candle Creek is above the treeline and above the Arctic Circle, so there are only low growing blueberry bushes and clumps of tundra grass between areas of wet bog in the summer from thawing boggy earth. This hinders easy walking in the spring. Wagons use skids to navigate tundra and bog in the summer.

(Top) Winter outing for Candle residents. (Middle) Winter freight delivery. (Bottom) Winter mail delivery.

Supplies in summer were brought from Kiwalik (which sat at the mouth of the river) by small coastwise vessels from Nome or by the larger freighters direct from San Francisco or Seattle. In summer the mail was brought from Nome by a small coastal vessel, on a two or three week schedule, which might be lengthened to nearly a month by unfavorable conditions. In winter communication and transportation of the mail was by dog team, and the mail was on a two week schedule.

In the winter sleds and dogs or reindeer were used exclusively for transportation. Candle was the turnaround point for the first major mushing competition in 1908, the All Alaska Sweepstakes, which ran 408 miles from Nome to Candle and back. Winter was a much easier time of year to get around. So many of us had our dogs and sleds. I mastered this skill right away and could travel in winter to other villages. I had a dog team of five Malamutes and a lead dog named "Quick" that was mostly Newfoundland. They were harnessed to a dog sled that had a brake on the back that drove thru hard snow while I stood on the back of the runners that extended about 8 inches behind the sled.

My lead dog "Quick," shortly after my arrival in Candle Creek, adopted me. He was brought into Alaska by a girl named Lizzie as a puppy and was taught to lead in a dog team. I was out picking blueberries one day and this dog would always watch me from the neighbor's house and would move closer as I moved along. I asked his owner why the dog watched me and he said he used to belong to a girl who went "outside" so he wants to get acquainted. He said that the dog's name was Quick. So the next day as the dog watched me I said, "Come Quick," and he came on the run to me! He went home with me and never left. My husband told the man that he had better sell him because the dog didn't want to leave my side. So we made a deal of $10.00 on the next "clean up," and he then belonged to me.

Stella & Quick.

K Arthur & Stella (Mama)

Winter sod homes

He was so smart and understood all commands such as "gee" to turn right, "haw" to turn left, "mush" to go, and "whoa" to stop. He didn't care too much about being hitched up, but would rather run free. Sometimes if he came into the house and he heard me say, "I think I will hitch up Quick and go for a ride," he would go out and run and hide until feeding time. He was about four years old when he adopted me.

The Malamutes have heavy fur and a bushy tail. They don't like to sleep in a dog house. They will often eat their way out to sleep outside, where they sleep in a coil with their nose under their tail to keep it from freezing. Our cabin at the claim had a sod roof and was built into a tundra hillside. The dogs would walk up the tundra and sleep around the chimney. Sometimes they would get covered with snow and yet they stayed nice and warm.

I took a ride with my son and sled dogs every day that it did not storm. If I met another team on the trail I was pretty sure of a dog fight. I stood at my sled, while the other musher, generally a man, parted them with his whip so I could go on my way. I was one of the few women who drove dogs. One man called me "The Rough Rider". I developed pretty good leg muscles by getting off and mushing behind the sled.

There was an abundance of salmon in the creek which we caught in the short summers, dried in the sun, and saved for winter. The pink salmon (that we referred to as dog salmon) we dried for the dogs and the red salmon we kept for ourselves.

I took good care of my dogs by cooking for them. I would cook rice in a five gallon coal oil can and when the rice was done I cut up dog salmon into it while it was hot. The dogs loved it. Most people only fed their dogs dried dog salmon but they get really tired of that. My dogs were fat and liked me, so they minded me well.

The weather was very unpredictable in winter, so blizzards can suddenly appear. Once when my son was about six months old, he and I were out with our sled and dog team visiting a friend in a neighboring village. On our return to Candle just such a blizzard caught me by surprise. Suddenly there was a complete whiteout. I knew that if we took the wrong turn and didn't make it home quite soon we would both freeze to death. I was so fortunate to have such a wonderful lead dog. I frantically commanded, "Quick, take us home", and at that command he took charge, leading five other dogs into the wind and ice and very thankfully got us home safe and sound. He ate very well that night!

Ed (Pop), Quick & K Arthur, Out for a stroll.

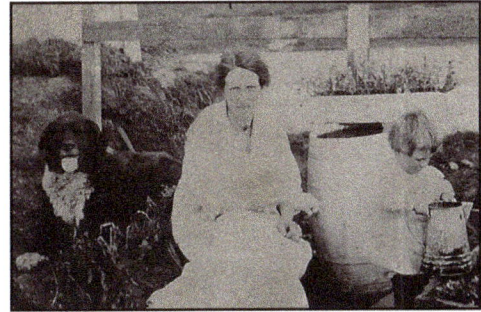
Quick, K Arthur & Stella watering garden.

Quick & K Arthur.

Quick had a reputation for being able to fight and protect himself from the Malamutes that tend to run in packs. A man told me he saw Quick one time whip five dogs by backing up to a building and grabbing them, one by one, by the neck and throwing them until they gave up and left. But it seems like these Malamutes remember dogs that whip them. So, one day they met Quick on the trail and they attacked him. A neighbor saw the five dogs fighting Quick and tried to stop them, but they had already killed him by breaking his back. The neighbor threw him down an empty mine shaft. I felt so bad to lose such a good faithful dog that I cried for a week.

Supplies had to be arranged for a year in advance. If a family had planned to leave Alaska and if the creek did not melt or leaving was not an option, miners' families would pool their resources to get the family through the winter till the following spring.

We raised a garden of various vegetables in wooden boxes above ground in the summer. The permafrost kept us from planting below ground. Because of the continual sunshine things grew very rapidly. We also had an abundance of wild blueberries which we really appreciated and put to good use.

We depended on each other in the community and we also created our own fun. I liked to write, so we would put on plays and everyone would attend. We held dances and card parties and in summer would stay up till three A.M. and go home with the sun still up!

K Arthur & Edward (Pop)

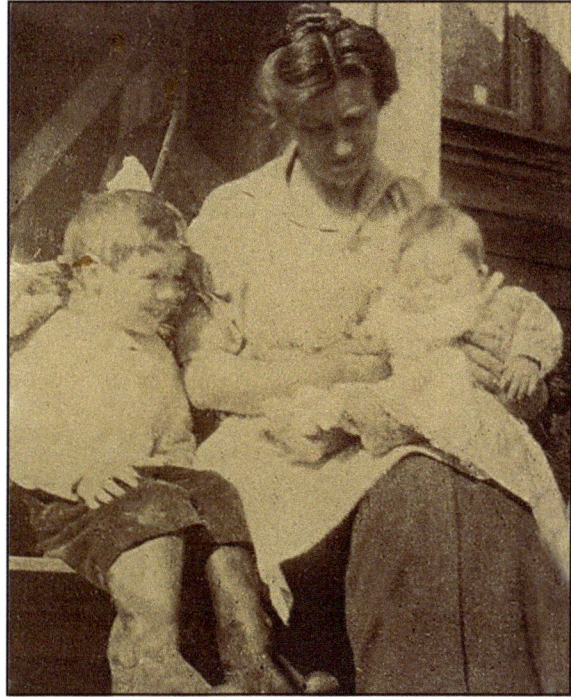

K Arthur, Lola & Stella (Mama)

K Arthur, Lola & Pop.

Stella, Lola & K Arthur.

Stella & Pals.

One of our memorable visitors was Roald Amundsen, the famous explorer from Norway who drove a dog team through Candle Creek on his way to the North Pole. We held a dance in his honor and I was even able to dance the Virginia reel with him! The next day I had him in my home for lunch. He did not make it to the North Pole at that time, which was, I believe, 1922, but later achieved his goal by airplane in 1925. We were so sorry to hear later that he had disappeared while searching for a friend in 1928.

Roald Amundsen

Norwegian explorer

Born July 1872

Disappeared June 1928

Age 55

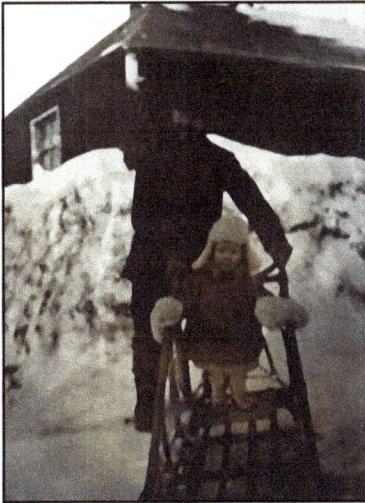

"Mush!"

Two shoveling stiffs in front of
sod home.

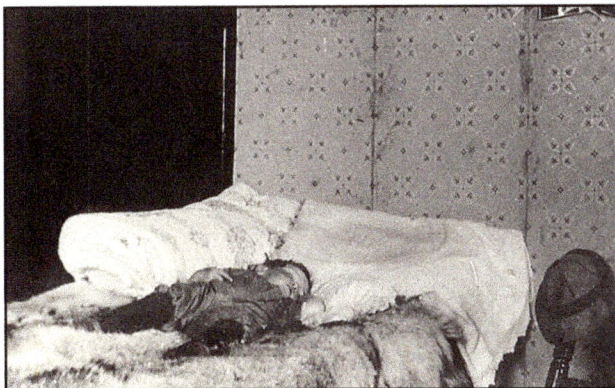

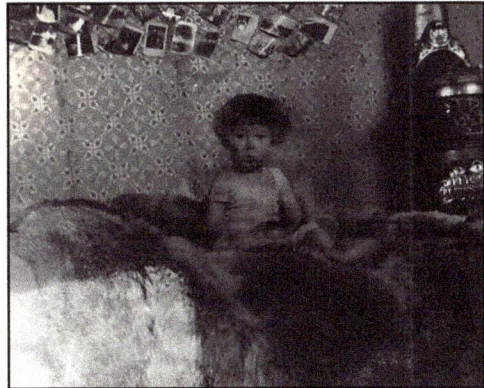

Inside summer home.

Our summer homes were very simple and hard to keep warm, having only small pot-bellied stoves. On our claim up the Candle Creek we had a dugout home with piled up sod and sod roof. This was snug and very warm in winter, when we kept a fire going day and night. I could even grow plants in the window in the winter, as it stayed so warm.

As there was no wood to be had for fuel we used local coal in our stoves for heat and cooking. Local coal was not very efficient, as it had a great deal of ice content. But it worked just the same.

Coal team hauling local coal.

Prospectors heading up river.

Klondike gold miners.

Wed. April 29, 1959 (Sec. 1)   Kent (Wn.) News-Journal   5

Here's How to Bake Sour-Dough Bread — The Alaskan Way!

Mrs. Stella Fox, 24011 94th Ave. has had a receipe for Sour-Dough Bread, accepted for publication in the Century 21 cookbook called "the Sourdough Bean-Pot."

This cook book will be printed in 1960 by the Alaska Friends, a ladies' club in Seattle, whose members are all former residents of Alaska. Mrs. Fox is an active member of this organization. The club owns and maintains a home at 6741 Beacon Ave., Seattle, for elderly members of the group.

As a tribute to Yukon- Alaska Pioneers, they are gathering receipes and anecdotes for the cookbook.

Mrs. Fox pioneered in t h e Arctic region for several years in her early married life, and her son and daughter were born at Candle, Alaska, a gold-mining town.

This is the Original Recipe of 1898 for Sour-dough bread; operating in the black.

"If you have any flour, take 1 cupful, add 2 cups of warm, melted snow-water, a spread sugar or molasses. Stir thoroughly in a coffee can, then set it behind the stove, on a box. Leave it there for two or three days, or until it "works." If you are fortunate enough to have a yeast cake, then it will w o r k much faster. If it freezes in the cabin, at night, take it to bed with you, preferably under an antique wolf-robe.

In due time find a wooden pickle bucket, to be used permanently. Cook up a big mess of dehydrated potatoes; use all of the water and some of t h e potatoes. Add enough flour to make a big batch of sponge. Add some more sugar and return it behind the stove.

If you want pancakes first, then take out most of the sponge leaving enough in the bucket for a good "starter." Add some soda to sweeten, a spoonful of salt and some more sugar or blackstrap molasses, some b a c o n grease, and a couple of tablespoons of soaked, dried eggs.

Next, grease the top of the stove well, and dip the batter onto the stove to fry in nine-inch cakes. If you have no butter, use molasses, or sugar-syrup to decorate, then eat.

For the bread: Continue process as given above for sponge, let rise overnight, using precaution, as mentioned, if freezing temperature around 32 to 52 degrees below zero.

In the early morning, add soda, salt, grease and enough flour to knead stiff. Place in a dishpan and let rise until double in bulk. Make into loaves and let rise again.

Bake the loaves for an hour, but don't let the stove get red-hot.

A real, old "Sourdough" does not bother to wash the mixing pan, but hangs it on the wall till the next baking day. When the wooden bucket gets a layer of dough, about 1 or 2-inches thick around the sides, t h e n your dough has reached t h e height of Sourdough perfection, and has attained the healthful consistency of the original penicillin. Then you will know that you have reached the climax of a professional "Sour-d o u g h Bread-maker."

Mrs. Fox's note at the end of t h e receipe says: "Any old Alaskan Sourdough" will vouch for the workability of this receipe."

With the interior of our homes getting cooler at night in winter, we had a problem keeping our sourdough "starter" alive. But we had a solution to this problem, by taking it to bed with us!

In winter there was no problem keeping game and food stored. We would have a hole in the ground, lined with furs, and something heavy on the top to keep the dogs out. This worked for us much like a modern freezer!

When my son was about six months old, in the winter of 1912, I heard of a contest that the Kellogg's company of Battle Creek, Michigan was having. They wanted stories and a photograph from families using Kellogg's corn flakes from remote locations. I proceeded to take a picture as shown here with our sleigh, lead dog Quick, my son and a big box of Kellogg's corn flakes. About a year later I received a letter of apology stating that we would have been a sure winner, however the letter and photo arrived too late for the contest entry date!

K Arthur, Quick & Kellogg's Corn Flakes.

Stella on the windless.

K Arthur dressed in fur.

Edward A. Fox on #14 claim.

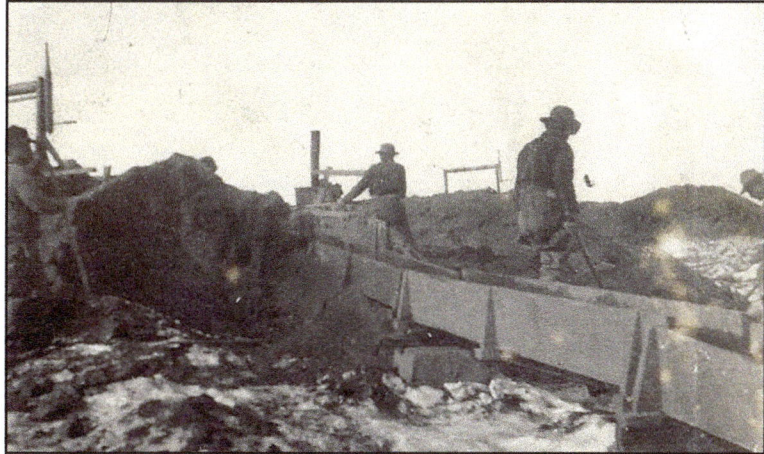

Sluicing scene.

Hydraulic mining on Bull Hill.

Cabin on #11 claim.

By the spring of 1911 the easier to find placer gold, found in the stream beds after being eroded out of bedrock, was virtually played out. So the method used then was called open cut and drift mining. Drift miners worked underground in the winter, thawing the earth with fires, or steam, hauling it to the surface to wait for spring. When the creeks thawed they washed the gold out of the tons of earth by diverting the water into sluices, which were long wooden boxes. The boxes had wooden slats nailed to the bottom to catch the gold. Rocker boxes were also used to sift out the finer gold.

Hydraulic mining was a more efficient method when gold became more difficult to find, unfortunately it was more damaging to the landscape.

Later large mining conglomerates leased or bought up claims for hydraulic mining and built dredging rigs on the rivers.

As the gold in the area of Candle Creek became depleted and more difficult to find, we made plans to move the family to the Seattle, Washington area in the fall of 1923. In preparation for that move we had to do something that was very difficult. We could not sell our dogs as no one needed them, and if we left them behind, they would starve. My husband had to take them out and shoot them. Even more heartbreaking was when a few hours later one of the dogs, having only been grazed on the head by the bullet, returned to the house and had to be put down a second time. This was very hard, as they had served us so well.

We had an early freeze that fall and leaving Candle Creek became a problem. Our party of 14 men, women and children had to to walk overland to get to the coast where we were to board the clipper ship that would take us to Seattle. Upon arriving in Kotzebue Sound, after an arduous trip, we found the harbor froze in, which made it impossible for us to sail. The U.S. Coast Guard was contacted for an emergency rescue and as you can see by the newspaper clipping and radiogram that I have kept all these years, we were successfully rescued by the US Coast Guard ship *Algonquin*. I also took one photo during the 20 mile trip, by small rescue boats, to the ship.

ARGONAUTS OF ARCTIC SAVED

Eleven Families Saved by Cutter Algonquin

Marooned Party on Verge of Starvation

Effort to Save Japanese Steamer Fails

First news of two of the most unusual and thrilling rescues ever effected in the ice-bound Arctic was brought to Los Angeles Harbor yesterday by the U.S.S. Algonquin, United States Coast Guard cutter, adding another absorbing chapter to the never-ending romance of the coast guard service in Alaskan waters. The Algonquin is here for winter station and complete overhaul after completing a 19,000-mile patrol cruise in seven months up under the Arctic Circle.

She herself brought the news of her rescue of eleven gold miners and their families from Kotzebue Sound, on the North Alaska coast, after they had been marooned by the Arctic winter. News of their plight reached the Algonquin through the act of one of their number in hiking 100 miles over the mountains to the nearest telegraph station.

NEAR STARVATION

The stranded argonauts, near starvation when the Algonquin reached them, had to be transported eleven miles in small boats to the Algonquin, the ice and reefs of Kotzebue Sound preventing the craft from reaching them.

The Algonquin reached Nome with the eleven families on October 28 and immediately headed south for winter quarters—already having overstayed her season. But shortly after getting underway radio distress signals were picked up from the Japanese steamer Shinkoku Maru, reporting herself with a broken tail shaft and helpless in a storm in latitude 51 north, longitude 162 west. The Algonquin reached her on November 4, got a line aboard and started against the gale for St. Paul, Alaska. The storm increased and on November 7 the hawser parted twice under the tremendous strain of the 10,000-ton freighter, finally disabling the towing machinery and towing rail of the Algonquin so seriously that she was forced to cast off and radio for assistance.

SHIP TOTAL LOSS

A week later the tug Numaconna reached the scene from Seattle, but after fighting the storm for twelve days and night, the 1500-horse-power tug was herself forced to cast off the helpless vessel. That night the Shinkoku Maru was driven ashore on Montague Island, a total loss.

During her record cruise the Algonquin operated from the northern end of Alaska, south to Bristol Bay and westward to Attu, the very tip of the Aleutian Islands chain, and the westermost contiguous possession of the United States. In addition to the two above instances, the Algonquin last summer rescued nearly a score of stranded and helpless craft of the Alaskan fishing fleet.

She is in command of Lieutenant-Commander E. A. Coffin, a veteran officer of the coast guard in Alaska, and carries a crew of sixty men.

Saved From Death by Coast Guard Cutter

Rescued Miners and Their Families

Escape starvation on Alaska shore, where they were marooned 135 miles north of the Arctic Circle.

Front left K Arthur, then Stella with husband Edward behind..

ALGONQUIN SAVES LIVES OF STRANDED

Coast Guard Cutter Braves Dangers of Arctic Ocean To Go To Relief of Helpless.

DISABLED SHIP IS AIDED

Completing Fifteen-Thousand Mile Cruise In Alaskan Waters, Captain Gabbett Is Nearing End of Season of Real Service to Residents of The Northland.

The United States coast guard cutter Algonquin, Captain Cecil M. Gabbert in command, is daily expected to arrive in Seattle, completing a fifteen-thousand mile cruise this season through Southeastern Alaska, as far as Attu island, of the Aleutian group of islands and north to the Arctic circle. The Algonquin is the first government steel vessel to cruise above the Arctic circle this late in the year.

The Algonquin has a record of achievement in the way of life and property saving of which the master has reason to be proud.

While the coast guard vessel was anchored at Nome, October 17, Captain Gabbett received information that the American gas boat Silver Wave, with passengers, including women and children, was fourteen days overdue while enroute from Nome to Kotzebue. The last heard of the Silver Wave was that it was off Cape Prince of Wales. It was believed at Nome that the boat was lost. Taking on board a power life-saving boat from the Nome life saving station, the Algonquin proceeded at full speed in search of the missing craft. On the afternoon of October 18, the Silver Wave was located at Port Clarence. The gas boat had been as far north as Shismaref inlet, but was forced to turn back on account of strong gales and rough weather. Whereupon, the Algonquin proceeded through Bering strait and into the Arctic ocean to Kotzebue, to the rescue of seven men, two women and five children who were stranded there. Transportation had stopped for the season, winter supplies had not been received and some of the stranded people were in need of medical aid, which was promptly provided.

On October 19, the Algonquin anchored at Kotzebue, and sent a life-saving boat a distance of twenty miles, in a rough sea, and brought off fourteen stranded people. They were cold, wet and in an exhausted condition. The party, which included women and children, had traveled all night, on foot, the baggage, being transported by dog team. The party had taken along lumber to build crude bridges over streams, in the trip from the interior to the sea coast, and experienced hardships severe and trying in the extreme, especially for the women and children. Such crucial relief work by the coast guard cutter not only won the gratitude of the stranded people who had been saved, but won the praises of the people of the extreme Northland who heard of the heroic rescue work.

Among the rescued were C. F. Weinard, of the Kewalik Mining Company, and family, who were taken to Nome. They will arrive in Seattle on the steamer Buford, soon due.

While enroute from the Arctic to Seattle, the Algonquin went to the rescue of the disabled Japanese freighter Shinkoku Mary, off the Aleutian islands, in Southwestern Alaska. The helpless vessel was towed to Dutch harbor by the cutter.

The Algonquin has on board a number of live female fur seal, the first to be brought outside for many years.

The 20 mile boat ride to the U.S. Coast Guard ship *Algonquin*.

Arrival of the U.S. Coast Guard *Algonquin* rescue ship to port of Seattle.

TREASURY DEPARTMENT,
U. S. COAST GUARD.
Form 2655—Ed. 10,000—Sept. 1921.

U. S. COAST GUARD RADIO SERVICE

S. R. S. No. **50**

FILED U.S.C.G.C. ALGONQUIN   POSITION SEA   DATE 10 21 23   19

PREFIX	ORIGIN	NO.	OPERATOR	CHECK	TIME FILED
C. O.			SEND.	RECG.	

RADIO   RADIO   ALGONQUIN   322   GOVT.   DATE

GOVT.

OCTOBER 20 1923 KIWALIK KOTZEBUE SOUND ARCTIC OCEAN DASH COAST GUARD CUTTER ALGONQUIN ANCHORED NOME ALASKA SEVENTEENTH RECEIVED INFORMATION AMERICAN GAS SCHOONER SILVER WAVE WITH PASSENGERS INCLUDING WOMEN AND CHILDREN FOURTEEN DAYS OVERDUE NOME TO KOTZEBUE LAST HEARD FROM OFF CAPE PRINCE OF WALES BELIEVED LOST PERIOD RECEIVED POWER LIFESAVING BOAT ON BOARD FROM NOME STATION PROCEEDED AT FULL SPEED IN SEARCH OF HER PERIOD AFTERNOON EIGHTEENTH FOUND SILVER WAVE IN PORT CLARENCE HAVING BEEN AS FAR AS SHISHMAREF INLET AND FORCED TO TURN BACK BY STRONG GALES AND STORMY WEATHER PERIOD PROCEEDING THROUGH BERING STRAITS AND INTO ARCTIC OCEAN TO KOTZEBUE TO RESCUE OF SEVEN MINERS TWO WOMEN AND FIVE CHILDREN STRANDED THERE PERIOD TRANSPORTATION STOPPED WINTER SUPPLIES NOT RECEIVED AND IN NEED OF MEDICAL AID PERIOD TEMPERATURE AT CANDLE FIVE DEGREES ABOVE ZERO RIVERS FROZEN AND ALL MINING STOPPED ALGONQUIN FIRST STEEL GOVERNMENT VESSEL TO CRUISE ABOVE ARCTIC CIRCLE THIS LATE IN THE YEAR ON ACCOUNT OF DESCENDING ICE FLOWS

SENT   TO   DATE   TIME

VIA

FOR RADIOGRAMS OTHER THAN COMMERCIAL   IF THIS MESSAGE IS NOT DESTINED BEYOND THE COAST GUARD RADIO SERVICE THE PREFIX AND WORD "GOVT." IN ADDRESS SHALL NOT BE TRANSMITTED. USE OTHER SIDE IF NECESSARY.

Description of the U.S. Coast Guard ship *Algonquin* rescue of stranded families in Kotzebue Sound.

PERIOD NINETEENTH INSTANT ANCHORED IN KOTZEBUE SOUND AND SENT LIFE-SAVING BOAT TWENTY MILES IN ROUGH SEA AND BROUGHT OFF FOURTEEN STRANDED PEOPLE WET AND IN EXHAUSTED CONDITION BUT GRATEFUL TO THE COAST GUARD PERIOD THE WOMEN AND CHILDREN HAD TRAVELED ALL NIGHT ON FOOT BAGGAGE BROUGHT ON DOG SLED LUMBER BROUGHT ALONG AND BRIDGES BUILT ENROUTE TO SEA COAST EXPERIENCED HARDSHIPS UNKNOWN PERIOD THIS CRUCIAL RELIEF WORK DAILY EXPERIANCE OF COAST GUARD STOP C F WEINARD AND FAMILY KIWALIK MINING COMPANY PIONEER BUILDING SEATTLE AMONG THOSE RESCUED FOR TRANSPORTATION TO STATES VIA STEAMER BUFORD LAST VESSEL FROM NOME STOP ARRIVE TWENTY SECOND STOP ALGONQUIN EXPECTS ARRIVE SEATTLE ABOUT NOVEMBER TENTH AFTER EIGHTEEN THOUSAND MILES CRUISE THROUGH SOUTH EAST ALASKA FAR WEST AS ATTU ISLAND ALEUTIAN ISLANDS AND NORTH TO ARCTIC CIRCLE STOP WILL BRING LIVE FEMALE FUR SEALS FIRST SEEN SEATTLE IN MANY YEARS FURTHER INFORMATION CRUISE CALL COAST GUARD PIONEER BUILDING SEATTLE

ALGONQUIN

Stella, Edward & K Arthur (far right) visiting Tijuana, Mexico, 1915.

Upon arriving in Seattle we settled just south in Kent, Washington where we purchased a five acre chicken farm complete with a house and barn. We also purchased a new car. Some might say that we were not a great success in our mining venture, but we made a living for some twelve years, visited the lower 48 states several times, and made a family vacation to Mexico in 1915. In 1918 I made a trip outside to my hometown of Plainfield, Iowa with my son and daughter.

We were never rich, but never poor. Because we lived on a small farm and could raise a great deal of what we needed, we survived the Great Depression in good shape. We raised an abundance of corn, vegetables, had a small apple orchard and raised a lot of chickens.

After settling in Kent, Washington, I was able to take a correspondence course in "Silent screen writing classes," which in 1924 turned out to be just a bit late, as "talkies" came out in 1927!

Edward continued to return to Alaska in the summers with our son K Arthur to work for larger mining companies, mostly in the Fairbanks area, while Lola and I remained on the farm until Arthur was 25 years old in 1937.

K Arthur Fox & "Big Bertha" hydraulic mining.

Edward A. Fox 1932

Steam pipes to melt the permafrost.

K Arthur Fox, melting the permafrost.

Going home after a hard days work.

River gold dredge.

Salaries in Alaska Are Very High

But a T-Bone Steak Costs $4.50 and a Suit of Clothes $150—Principal Industry is Gold Mining Carried on Only During Summer.

Oct. 1934

IMAGINE, if you can, sitting down to a T-bone steak that is none too juicy, fully aware that when the last morsel has been swallowed you are going to be assessed $4.50 for the meal, and enjoying it. That price would make even caviar taste flat.

Yet, says Arthur Fox, Fairbanks, Alaska, that is what the citizens of the north country with a yen for T-bone steaks must hand the cashier when they have satisfied their cravings.

At the current rate of exchange the price would buy all the T-bones in the largest slaughtered cornfed beef and would almost buy the whole critter on the hoof from farms of drouth stricken livestock men.

Of course, not all meals are so high, Mr. Fox hastens to explain. The "ordinary" victuals are quite cheap, the "average" meal costing only $1.50 per each, about 15 cents a forkful.

Alaskans, though, do not consider the prices exhorbitant. Wages are high, riches come and go in the twinkling of an eye and besides practically all of their foodstuffs have to be imported from the United States or Canada.

Such commonplace things as depressions have never been known, except after a major catastrophe such as fire or freakish weather that may lay waste entire towns or cut off the means of supply. Principle industry is gold—the magic metal that lured Arthur's father, E. A. Fox, into the country with other prospectors in 1897—and price of the money metal has seldom fluctuated, except this year when President Roosevelt and his New Dealers sent the price soaring and a great boom struck the distant land.

Alaska also had no need for the NRA and its multidinuous bureaus and investigators attempting to raise the salaries of the working man. Most common of common labor, Arthur says, like the workers on the railroad, are paid $105 per month and their board and room. Arthur, who has a more skilled job, setting water points in a gold mine, finds $200 in his pay envelope at the end of every month and boards and rooms at the expense of the F-E company. All jobs are contracted for "with board and room."

Clothing, too, is relatively high. A "hand-me-down" suit of clothes will cost about $50 or $75 but "tailored made" suits average around the $150 mark and Alaskans, schooled in the rigors of the wild north will have nothing but the best. "It doesn't pay," says Arthur, born and reared in a small mining town north of Fairbanks.

While most of the foodstuffs and all clothing, etc., are imported a few farmers have drifted in and manage to raise megre crops during the short Alaskan summer. "What is planted grows fast," Arthur explained. "Quite a lot of spuds are raised but they aren't very good. Too much water. When they are cooked nothing remains but water and a few shriveled potatoes about the size of peas."

Hot houses raise some of the smaller fruits and vegetables, but great prices are demanded. A box of "home grown" strawberries may be bought for 50 cents a pint if you must have your strawberries and cream—canned cream.

But with salaries high and gold to be found along the many creeks flowing out of mountains on the flat plains surrounding Fairbanks the Alaskans don't mind. Most of them work for the F-E (Fairbanks Exploration) company whose placer mines stretch for miles in every direction. It is the most powerful organization in those parts.

But mining is possible only during the summer months when roads are open and no snow or ice is on the ground. Comes winter and the miners either gather up their traps and take the long hike into the McKinley Park region to trap for furs or take the boat to Seattle and the United States.

Trapping has not been highly remunerative in past years and most of the miners have, like Arthur and his family, come into the United States. Almost overnight Fairbanks, a bustling city of 5,000 in the summer, shrinks until only 2,500-3,000 remain to spend the long winter.

Even in summer time—unprecedented heat of 87 above was registered last summer—mining is done under difficulty. The ground seldom thaws more than a foot below surface and artificial means must be called upon to thaw the frozen turf before being dredged and sluiced.

The F-E company uses cold water, sinking pipes to bed rock at 16-foot intervals and then forcing cold water through them into the ground until the soil is loosened. Smaller operators with less capital use steam but it is expensive.

The gold is all free-gold and few smelters are necessary. Power is steam as coal is plentiful and easy to get. What electricity there is comes from steam turbines as water power is inaccessible most of the year.

Although railroads have penetrated far into Alaska rates are high—ranging from six cents a mile to 25 cents a mile for each person—and the prevailing mode of transportation is the airplane. Especially in winter is the Wright brothers contribution to civilization needed. Then, when roads are blocked and those citizens who own cars have jacked them up in garages and dog teams are the only means of transportation, the airplane soars about at will, landing almost any place on the frozen snow.

Fairbanks has a modern high school and a daily newspaper. Outside of basketball and a little hockey and the annual Fourth of July baseball game there are not many sports. Picture shows and other amusements as we know them here abound.

Although but 22 years old, Arthur has been working in the mines for five years and has trapped in and beyond McKinley park. In fact, to use his own words, "I have been in almost every part of Alaska at some time or another." And he plans to go back there next spring.

Arthur with a friend, Bruce Ward, visited at the John Sherwood home in Nebraska City this fall en route to Tennessee where Ward's parents live. Arthur's mother is a sister of Mrs. Sherwood, was born in the Midwest and lived here much of her life. She met E. A. Fox in California, married him and accompanied him into Alaska in search of gold and riches. They now reside in Seattle, Washington, although Arthur and his father make the annual trek into the north every summer.

Mrs. Fox has a coin carried across the North Pole by Amundsen, the great explorer who flew in the "Norge" across the northern tip of the world. Amundsen dined on several occasions at the Fox home during his many Arctic expeditions.

Edward A. Fox (Pop) & K Arthur Fox, 1934.

Recognition Given Kent Woman on Freedom Letter

A letter written by Mrs. Stella Fox, Route 3, Box 15, was read over the U. S. State Department "Voice of America" program Tuesday morning.

Mrs. Fox submitted the letter through a national radio program. It dealt with the theme of freedom in America.

For submitting a letter which was chosen to be read over "Voice of America," Mrs. Fox was awarded a small, gold pin by the sponsors of the program through which she submitted the letter.

In the '40s, during World War II, I was able to again use my teaching experience when I taught adult night school citizenship classes. This I found very rewarding.

In 1951 I submitted a letter through a national radio program. It dealt with the theme of "Freedom in America." My letter was chosen to be read on the radio program "Voice of America", and I also received a gold pin and a letter of recognition from the Mutual Broadcasting System, signed by Gabriel Heatter, a noted radio journalist and announcer. It aired Feb. 27, 1951.

February 17, 1951

Mrs. Stella Fox
Route 3, Box 15
Kent, Wash.

Dear Mrs. Fox:

One of the most precious assets of our nation lies in
its great number of citizens who "do something about it"
when a national question arises. It is this spirit which
accounts for our splendid community movements and which,
in real measure, has made us a free democracy.

The offices of the State Department, which cooperated
with me and the Mutual Broadcasting System in the VOICES OF
AMERICA campaign, have selected your letter to be broadcast
to the people of the world over the Voice of America facil-
ities. May I offer my sincerest congratulations on your
splendid letter. I know that it came right from the heart
and from all the pride and thanksgiving you feel for this
glorious free democracy.

I take great pleasure, on behalf of myself, the Mutual
Broadcasting System and the Voice of America, in presenting
you with the enclosed commemorative pin which will be worn
by only those listeners whose contributions were selected.
I hope that you will accept and wear this pin as a real
badge of honor.

With best wishes of the season,

Cordially yours,

Gabriel Heatter

P.S. Your letter will be broadcast on February 27, 1951.

My son K Arthur and his wife Arlis returned to Candle Creek by bush pilot aircraft to visit his boyhood home in the mid 1970s finding little change after 50 years. Many of the buildings remained standing, including the Fairhaven Hospital building. It was nearly a ghost town except for an old boyhood friend of K Arthur's, with his wife and nephew. A lot of the old equipment was right where it had been used 50 years before and was very well preserved, the weather being so cold and dry.

K Arthur commented of his boyhood home, "As far as the eye can reach, with no fences, autos, humans or roads to mar this vast wilderness, only the birds, wild animals, wind and running water sounds may be heard. Candle, Alaska, "America's Last Frontier".

K Arthur & daughter Kay L. Clark & husband Joseph F. Clark.

K Arthur & wife Arlis M. Fox.

Fairhaven Hospital, Candle, Alaska, 1970s.

They flew back a couple of years later, this time bringing along their eldest daughter and husband, spending a week camping out in an old abandoned cabin, having brought with them a foot locker of necessary supplies.

My husband Edward suffered a brain hemorrhage and passed away in Kent, Washington, in 1951, at the age of 77. My daughter Lola preceded me in death in 1975. I cared for her for 58 years. I moved to Chico, California, to be near my son K Arthur and family in 1975. At this time I am 96 years old.

The sad part of living a long life is that you outlive all of your old friends.

I do miss my Alaskan companions. … Once a sourdough, *always a sourdough!*

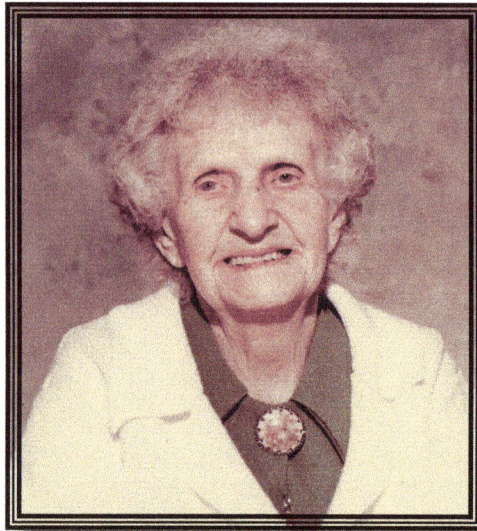

Stella Holmes Fox passed away March 1976, just one month short of her 97th birthday, during a gall bladder surgery in Chico, California. She was survived by her son K Arthur Fox, daughter-in-law Arlis M. Fox, three Granddaughters and three Great Grandsons.

Stella was:

- A charter member of the Waterloo, Iowa, branch of "The Daughters of the Grand Army of the Republic".
- A 60 year member of "The Alaska Yukon Pioneers Club".
- One of the last surviving members of the original Kent, Washington, "East Hill Helping Hand Club."

STELLA H. FOX
1879 ——— 1976

PROOF OF LABOR

United States of America)
) S S

Territory of America   )

                     E,A,Fox being duly sworn on oath deposes,

and says:

That for the year ending December31,1920. at least ONE HUNDRED DOLLERS

worth of labor was performed ^on and for the benifet of each of the following

described Placer Mining Claims.

Situated in ~~in~~ the Fairhaven Recording Precinct,,Territory of Alaska, towit':

No 15, Sec. Tier Bench L.L. Candle Creek Above Dis.

 No 12, First Tier Bench L.L. Candle Creek   "   " .

No11, First Tier Bench L.L.   ' ' ' ' ' ' '   " "

On 15, Work consisted of sinking ~~of taking~~ shaft to bedrock and drifting

with a boiler near north center side of claim. Said work was done from

Dec.10 1920 to Dec. 21,1920

On No11 work consisted of sinking shafts and drifting, taking out

dumps and sluicing same,,said work was done near center of claim

  during the months March,April, May, June,1920.

ON No12 work con sisted of ground sluicing,cuting sods, maintaining

  ditch, sinking three shafts, twoshafts to bed rock, said work was done

near ~~West~~ center end of claim. during the month of July and October,

   1920,   In addition over $2000. worth of work was done on No11

Bench, whitch is contiguous to, and joins this claim.

     Said work was of the value of over One Hundred Dollars on each

claim, and was done at the instante of the owners ^Agent with the help of one

and two men.

                 E A Fox

Subscribed and swdrn to before me this 11 day of Jan.   A.D. 1921

                 Sidney R Simson

     Notary Public for Alaska reciding at Candle

     My commission expires June 20 19~~~

Proof of Annual Assessment Work

UNITED STATES OF AMERICA,
DISTRICT OF ALASKA, } ss.

.... E. A. Fox .... being first duly sworn, on oath, says:

That during the year ending December 31st, 1913, at least one hundred dollars worth of labor was performed and

improvements made on or for the benefit and development of the No. 15 2d tier bench

No. 11 1st tier both left limit placer mining claim, containing an area of less than twenty

acres, situated on Candle Creek

in the Fairhaven Mining and Recording District, District of Alaska.

That 20 worse days was done on said claim by affiant and one man on

No. 15 consisting of sinking shafts and drift-

on the following portion of said claim and consists of ing, during the months of J-

February and March, 1913 about the center of

the claim. On No. 11 20 days work by affiant

and one man sinking shafts and drifting

That said work was done on the following dates: during the month of

June, 1913 near the northeast corner of

claim

on each claim and was of the value of more than one hundred dollars.

That said work was done and improvements were made at the instance of R. H. Peterson

and S. Fox

That the actual amount paid for said work and improvements was two hundred

.... Dollars, and that said amount was paid by said R. H. Peterson

and S. Fox owner of said claims

E. A. Fox

Subscribed and sworn to before me this 20th day of March A. D., 1914

Notary Public for Alaska, residing at

#11976

Proof of Annual Assessment Work

CLAIM

....

....

....

....

....

DATED.................................... 191......

Recorded at the Request of

..E d Fox...

..Mch. 20.......... A. D., 1914

at.................min. past.........o'clock,

.............M., in Vol. 53

of Proofs of Labor, at page 171

Records of..Fairhaven

Recording Precinct.

..P J Heaston.......................

RECORDER.

By...

DEPUTY RECORDER.

Nugget Print.

Proof of Labor.

_____ C. S. Fox _____ being first duly sworn, say __s__:

That during the year ending December 31, 191_6_, at least one hundred dollars worth of labor was performed and improvements made on or for the benefit and development of _____ the

No 15   2nd Tier   Bench

No 11   1st Tier   Bench

No 12   1st Tier   Bench   all left limit

_____ placer mining claim_s_, situate

on Candle Cr.

in the _Fairhaven_ _____ Recording District, Territory of Alaska.

That _20_ _____ days work was done on _each_ of said claim_s_, consisting of

on No 15   Sluicing dumps & Ditching during

May & Sept 1916 with 1, 2, & three men

No 11   Drifting during Jan & Feb & Mch, 1916

with two men

No 12   ditching & sinking shafts during July

& sinking shafts in Oct 1916 near the

N. E. corner stake.

and was of the value of _over One Hundred_ Dollars _on Each Claim_

That said work was done _____ by _C. S. Fox_

& J. Wilkens

That said work was done and improvements were made at the instance of _R. H. Peterson_

owner of No 15–2nd Tier   C. S. Fox owner of No 12–1st Tier

& S. Fox owner of no 11–1st Tier Bench left limit Candle Cr

C. S. Fox

Subscribed and sworn to before me this _5th_ day of _March_ 191_7_

Geo D Humphrey

Notary Public for the Territory of Alaska.
My Commission Expires Sept. 1919,

PROOF OF ANNUAL LABOR—ALASKA PRINTING CO., NOME

Special Power of Attorney.

Know all men by these presents that I

Stella Fox of Candle, Alaska

have made, constituted and appointed, and by these presents does make, constitute and appoint

C S Fox of Candle, Alaska

My true and lawful attorney, for Me and in My name, place and stead,

to locate, stake, and Record quartz and Placer mining claims in Alaska. and having located the same to perform all necessary assessment Work thereon, and to bargain, sell, lease, work, release and convey the whole or any part thereof, to give deeds and deliver the same to any persons that my said attorney may see fit, and for any sum that he may see fit. thereby

Giving and Granting unto my said attorney full power and authority to do and perform all and every act and thing whatsoever requisite and necessary to be done in and about the premises, as fully to all intents and purposes as I might or could do if personally present, and I the said Stella Fox am hereby ratifying and confirming all that My said attorney C S Fox shall lawfully do or cause to be done by virtue of these presents.

In Witness Whereof, I have hereunto set My hand and seal the 29th day of April 1921.

Signed, sealed and delivered in the presence of

John Reddin

Stella Fox. (SEAL)

(SEAL)
(SEAL)
(SEAL)
(SEAL)
(SEAL)

SPECIAL POWER OF ATTORNEY

United States of America,
District of Alaska, ss.

Fairhaven Precinct

On this _29th_ day of _April_
A. D. One thousand nine hundred and _21_ personally came
before me, _E A Fox_ _U. S. Commissioner_
a Notary Public in and
for said District, the within named _Stella Fox_

to me personally known to be the identical person described within
and who executed the within instrument, and _she_
acknowledged to me that _she_ executed the same freely, for the
uses and purposes therein mentioned.

WITNESS my hand and seal this _29th_ day of
April 19_21_ _E A Fox_
Notary Public in and for the District of Alaska.

U. S. Commissioner
Fairhaven Precinct
Territory of Alaska.

#13479

Special Power of Attorney

Stella Fox

TO

E A Fox

DATED _Apr 27 1921_

Recorded at the Request of _E A Fox_

April 29th A. D. 1921
a _35_ min. pas _4_ o'clock,
P. M. in Vol. _41_
of Power of Attorney, at page _269_
Records of Fairhaven
Recording Precinct.

E A Fox
RECORDER.

By _J Tal. S. Ford_ DEPUTY RECORDER.

Placer Location Certificate.

I, the undersigned, having on the _31st_ day of _December_ 19_22_ discovered placer gold in the ground herein discribed, hereby claim for placer mining purposes the ground enclosed by a line running as follows,

Beginning at this Initial Stake, upon which a copy of this notice is posted and being the _South West_ Corner of said claim; running thence _660_ feet in a _Easterly_ direction to Stake No. 2, _S.E._ Corner, thence _2640_ feet in a _Northerly_ direction to Stake No. 3 _N.E._ Corner, thence _660_ feet in a _Westerly_ direction to stake No. 4, _N.W._ Corner, thence _2640_ feet in a _Southerly_ direction to the place of beginning.

This claim shall be known as _No. 10 above Discovery Group_ and is situated _on Canyon Creek_ _a Tributary of Buckland River_

in the _Fairhaven_ Mining District Territory of Alaska.

Date of the posting of this Notice on the claim _December 31_ 19_22_

C A Fox
S Stella Fox .... Locator**S**

(Revised and corrected May 1, 1918, and for sale by the NOME NUGGET.)—

NOTE FROM THE AUTHOR

I made my first cruise line voyage to Alaska in the summer of 1954 at the age of six years old, accompanied by my grandmother Stella and my twelve-year-old sister Kay. My grandmother wanted to show us her Alaska. I have so many wonderful memories of that trip that I will always cherish.

I had the opportunity to work aboard the S.S. *Universal Explorer*, cruising the inside passage, as a member of the beauty salon staff, for four summers 1998–2001. This gave me an even better view of the Far North firsthand.

I would never presume to call myself a "Sourdough," but can truly understand the passion of the pioneers for this land.

Since that experience I have had a driving desire to put my grandmother's words into print and share with others my Alaskan heritage.

—Sherry Fox Clark

www.ingramcontent.com/pod-product-compliance
Lightning Source LLC
Chambersburg PA
CBHW061415090426
42742CB00026B/3480